ideals®
CHRISTMAS

Wherever you go, wherever you are,
Keep in your heart the Christmas star;
Keep in your eyes the Christmas gleam,
And keep in your heart the Christmas dream;
May Faith, Hope, and Love mark your Christmas Day—
But keep each safe in your heart always.

—LESLIE-LEIGH DUCROS

IDEALS PUBLICATIONS

NASHVILLE, TENNESSEE

Christmastime

Linda Ann Hughes

*C*hristmas is a time for children. Children in stores, watching electric trains, gazing at beautiful bride dolls; children singing age-old Christmas carols; children playing in the snow; children whispering wonderful secrets . . .

Christmas is a midnight service, a Nativity scene of marble, gold, and jewels against a stained-glass sky. Christmas is a pageant, Tiny Tim, Scrooge, Merry Gentlemen, Noël, and a Silent Night. . . .

It's a time for decorations, streamers, bells, wreaths, mistletoe, holly, poinsettias, lights, and, best of all, a tree. The silver and gold trees are all very nice; but a real Christmas tree, well, there's just something about it, standing there proudly displaying its adornments. Some are beauties from faraway places; some are very, very old, brought out every year to take their places in the celebration, like the missing link uniting all the Christmases we've known. Other things change, but these old ornaments, our favorites, linger on. . . .

Add to this icicles, lights, and a star way up on top and you have a dream of a Christmas tree. Oh, yes, you also have the most wonderful fragrance in the world right in your living room. The decorations also include the family's Nativity scene, with its shepherds and their flocks, wise men, angels, Mary, Joseph, baby Jesus, all led by a star to a humble stable in Bethlehem where "the hopes and fears of all the years" await them.

Christmas is a time for good food: roast goose, cookies, nuts, eggnog, candy canes, apples, oranges, and fancy chocolates. It's a time for snow, Santa's helpers, reindeer, sleds, and a partridge in a pear tree.

Christmas is a heart-aching desire to be home for the holidays, and the ghost of Christmas past is never far away. It's a time for shopping lists, crowded streets, hustle, and bustle.

Christmas . . . "it came upon a midnight clear," and it lingers forever, leaving in its wake full hearts and the promise of a glorious and blessed New Year.

Brand-New World

Claire Mitchell

There's a brand-new world
   outside my door,
A world I've never seen before,
A pure white world no foot has trod,
A world that still belongs to God.

A reverent world, where even trees
Are offering prayers on bended knees,
Their heads bowed low, till sun's caress
Shall bid them rise, His name to bless.

This virgin world before me lies
To make my own through loving eyes;
I drink it deep, so deep, and then
I give it back to God again.

Acres of Diamonds

Faye Adams

The sun came up
today as usual,
but with a difference.

While we slept,
rain changed to snow,
quarter-size flakes
mounding on the wet earth.

Temperature dropped
faster than snowflakes,
freezing the garage door shut.

Morning brought
a crystal white cloak—
thousands of jewels,
winking in the sun.

A free gift
from the Diamond Maker.

Family ❧ Recipes

Christmas-Spiced Nuts

2 cups granulated sugar	½ teaspoon ground cloves
2 tablespoons ground cinnamon	3 egg whites
2 teaspoons ground ginger	2 tablespoons water
2 teaspoons grated orange peel	3 cups walnut halves
1 teaspoon salt	2 cups pecan halves
1 teaspoon ground nutmeg	1 cup whole unblanched almonds
1 teaspoon ground allspice	

Preheat oven to 300°F. In a medium bowl, combine first 8 ingredients; set aside. In a large bowl, beat egg whites and water until frothy. Add nuts; stir gently to coat. Add dry ingredients to nut mixture and stir gently to coat. Spread onto two large foil-lined baking sheets. Bake, uncovered, 20 to 25 minutes or until lightly browned, stirring every 10 minutes. Cool and serve. Makes 2 to 3 dozen servings.

Cocktail Meatballs

1 pound lean ground beef	1 14-ounce can jellied cranberry sauce
1 egg	¾ cup chili sauce
½ cup bread crumbs	1 tablespoon brown sugar
3 tablespoons minced onion	1½ teaspoons lemon juice
2 tablespoons water	

Preheat oven to 350°F. In a large bowl, mix together ground beef, egg, bread crumbs, minced onion, and water. Roll into small meatballs and place on baking sheet. Bake 20 to 25 minutes, turning once. In a slow cooker or large saucepan over low heat, blend the cranberry sauce, chili sauce, brown sugar, and lemon juice. Add meatballs and simmer for 1 hour before serving. Makes 10 servings.

Christmas Party Pinwheels

2 8-ounce packages cream cheese, softened
1 0.4-ounce package ranch salad dressing mix
½ cup minced red bell pepper
½ cup minced celery
¼ cup sliced green onions
¼ cup sliced pimiento-stuffed olives
3 to 4 10-inch flour tortillas

In a large bowl, beat cream cheese and dressing mix until smooth. Add red pepper, celery, onions and olives; mix well. Spread about ¾ cup on each tortilla. Roll up tightly; wrap in plastic wrap. Refrigerate for at least 2 hours. Cut into ½-inch slices. Makes 15–20 servings.

Holiday Brie en Croute

1 puff pastry sheet
⅓ cup dried cranberries
½ cup hot water
1 egg
1 tablespoon water
½ cup apricot preserves or raspberry jam
¼ cup toasted sliced almonds
1 8-ounce round Brie cheese
   Crackers

Thaw 1 pastry sheet according to package directions.

Preheat oven to 400°F. In a medium bowl, mix dried cranberries and ½ cup hot water. Let stand 1 minute. Drain and pat dry; set aside. In a small bowl, beat egg and 1 tablespoon water; set aside. Unfold pastry sheet on lightly floured surface. Roll into 13-inch square. Cut off corners to make a circle. Spread preserves to within 1 inch of pastry edge. Sprinkle cranberries and almonds over preserves. Top with cheese. Brush edge of pastry circle with egg mixture. Fold two opposite sides over cheese. Trim remaining two sides to 2 inches from edge of cheese. Fold these two sides onto the round. Press edges to seal. Place seam-side-down on baking sheet. Decorate top with pastry scraps if desired. Brush with remaining egg mixture. Bake 20 minutes or until golden. Let stand 45 minutes to 1 hour. Serve with crackers. Makes 12 servings.

Dorian Remine

From "Christmas"

Washington Irving

It is a beautiful arrangement . . . that this festival, which commemorates the announcement of the religion of peace and love, has been made the season for gathering together of family connections, and drawing closer again those bands of kindred hearts which the cares and pleasures and sorrows of the world are continually operating to cast loose; of calling back the children of a family who have launched forth in life and wandered widely asunder, once more to assemble about the paternal hearth, that rallying-place of the affections, there to grow young and loving again among the endearing mementoes of childhood.

There is something in the very season of the year that gives a charm to the festivity of Christmas. At other times we derive a great portion of our pleasures from the mere beauties of nature. Our feelings sally forth and dissipate themselves over the sunny landscape, and we "live abroad and everywhere." The song of the bird, the murmur of the stream, the breathing fragrance of spring, the soft voluptuousness of summer, the golden pomp of autumn; earth with its mantle of refreshing green, and heaven with its deep delicious blue and its cloudy magnificence, all fill us with mute but exquisite delight, and we revel in the luxury of mere sensation. But in the depth of winter, when nature lies despoiled of every charm and wrapped in her shroud of sheeted snow, we turn for our gratifications to moral sources. The dreariness and desolation of the landscape, the short gloomy days and darksome nights, while they circumscribe our wanderings, shut in our feelings also from rambling abroad, and make us more keenly disposed for the pleasures of the social circle. Our thoughts are more concentrated; our friendly sympathies more aroused. We feel more sensibly the charm of each other's society and are brought more closely together by dependence on each other for enjoyment. Heart calleth unto heart; and we draw our pleasures from the deep wells of living kindness, which lie in the quiet recesses of our bosoms and which, when resorted to, furnish forth the pure element of domestic felicity.

The pitchy gloom without makes the heart dilate on entering the room filled with the glow and warmth of the evening fire. The ruddy blaze diffuses an artificial summer and sunshine through the room and lights up each countenance into a kindlier welcome. Where does the honest face of hospitality expand into a broader and more heartfelt smile—where is the shy glance of love more sweetly eloquent—than by the winter fireside? And as the hollow blast of wintry wind rushes through the hall, claps the distant door, whistles about the casement, and rumbles down the chimney, what can be more grateful than that feeling of sober and sheltered security with which we look around upon the comfortable chamber and the scene of domestic hilarity? . . .

Photograph © GAP/SuperStock

The preparations making on every side for the social board that is again to unite friends and kindred; the presents of good cheer passing and repassing, those tokens of regard, and quickeners of kind feelings; the evergreens distributed about houses and churches, emblems of peace and gladness; all these have the most pleasing effect in producing fond associations, and kindling benevolent sympathies. . . .

Amidst the general call to happiness, the bustle of the spirits, and stir of the affections, which prevail at this period, what bosom can remain insensible? It is, indeed, the season of regenerated feeling—the season for kindling, not merely the fire of hospitality in the hall, but the genial flame of charity in the heart.

Prelude to Christmas

Clay Harrison

Tonight the world is white and silent
with freshly fallen snow.
Stars twinkle and shine like diamonds
above the village below.

There's gingerbread in the oven,
spiced cider, and pumpkin pie,
tasty echoes from yesteryear
when childhood friends stopped by.

Popcorn and cranberry garlands
are being strung with care,
and the fragrance of pine and cedar
permeate the frosty air.

Sleighbells ring in the distance;
all is calm and bright,
and nearby a church choir's singing
a soulful "Silent Night."

There are gifts beneath the
    Christmas tree,
decorations wall to wall,
and hopes are high as days pass by
that God will bless us all.

In the prelude to Christmas,
there is much to be done
as friends unite to celebrate
the coming of His Son.

It's Christmastime

Ruby Lee Mitchell

Carol singing, church bells ringing,
Once more Christmastime is here.
Children laughing, grownups beaming,
Hearts are warm with Christmas cheer.

Hearth fires glowing; look, it's snowing!
It will be quite deep by night;
And most everyone is saying,
"Lovely! Christmas will be white."

Pine and holly and mistletoe
Decking all the rooms and halls;
Tree lights gleam and firelight dancing
Flickers patterns on the walls.

Each snow-topped house warm and spicy,
Each gay heart just simply sings;
All the world is wrapped in beauty
With the joy that Christmas brings.

Christmas, Christmas, joyful season . . .
Warm reunions, love, and mirth;
And, oh, let each heart remember,
It's the holy Christ Child's birth.

Bits & Pieces

I want to wish you all the joy
Of happiness and cheer
That fills the heart of everyone
This festive time of year!

—*Esther Hirst*

A Christmas card is a singer of songs that tell an ancient story;
a holy night, nostalgic star, and heavenly angel's glory,
a card to be read, and read again . . .

—*Isabel Miller*

*C*hristmas is a gift from God that a man cannot
keep unless he gives it to someone else.

—*Dorothy Cameron Smith*

*T*here's something about a Christmas card,
At this season of the year,
Which leaves a special kind of joy
And fills the heart with cheer.

—*Alice Arlene MacCulloch*

Dorian Lee Ramine

A truly blessed Christmas
Is the gift I'm wishing you,
Filled with joy and laughter,
and with shining dreams come true.
—*Patricia Ann Emme*

*D*reams and hopes and wishes
Will all be coming true,
But best of all,
The ones you love
Are coming home to you!
—*Nelle Hardgrove*

*I*t isn't far to home, sweet home
When Christmas sights we see;
For we can always travel there
Though snowbound we might be.
—*Loise Pinkerton Fritz*

*C*hristmas cards from near and far
Seek my door as by a star,
But they are more than cards to me—
They're friends around my Christmas tree.
—*Ruth M. Bryan*

A Gingerbread House
Patricia Mongeau

Deep in the forest where all dreams come true
Is a gingerbread house just waiting for you.
Its roof is combined of sugar and spice,
And the chimney is made of everything nice.

Bright-colored bonbons grow round the front door,
And chocolate cookies are laid for the floor.
Its walls, made of cookies, are cheerful and gay,
And make this house seem like a nice place to stay.

The house is surrounded by green sugar trees,
And you may eat just as much as you please . . .
Deep in the forest where all dreams come true
Is a gingerbread house just waiting for you!

Gingerbread Memory
Pamela Love

I've lost count of the gingerbread houses
(Each perfect in every way)
That I've decorated in years past.
But what do I see today?

This marshmallow rooftop's collapsing;
That cinnamon chimney's askew.
The licorice windows are missing;
Quick—pass me icing for glue!

A dozen gumdrops have been squashed flat;
The sprinkles have spilled on my floor.
And I see only two or three candy canes
When there should be twice that or more.

But while judges may not give it prizes,
I'm prizing the giggles I hear.
With my grandchildren's help I am building
A gingerbread memory this year.

Our Treasured Traditions

FROM Christmas in Maine

Robert P. Tristram Coffin

If you want to have a Christmas like the one we had on Paradise Farm when I was a boy, you will have to hunt up a saltwater farm on the Maine coast, with bays on both sides of it, and a road that goes around all sorts of bays, up over Misery Hill and down, and through the fir trees so close together that they brush you and your horse on both cheeks. That is the only kind of place a Christmas like that grows. You must have a clear December night with blue Maine stars snapping like sapphires with the cold, and the big moon flooding full over Misery, and lighting up the snowy spruce boughs like crushed diamonds. . . .

I won't insist on your having a father like ours to drive you home to your Christmas. One with a wide moustache full of icicles and eyes like the stars of the morning. That would be impossible, anyway, for there has only been one of him in the world. But it is too bad, just the same. For you won't have the stories we had by the fireplace. . . .

But you will be able to have the rooms of the farmhouse banked with emerald jewels clustered on bayberry boughs, clumps of everlasting roses with gold spots in the middle of them, tree evergreens, and the evergreen that runs all over the Maine woods and every so often puts up a bunch of palm leaves. And there will be rose hips stuck in pine boughs. And caraway seeds in every crust and cookie in the place. . . . The Christmas tree will be there, and it will have a top so high that it will have to be bent over and run along the ceiling of the sitting room. It will be the best fir tree of the Paradise forests, picked from ten thousand almost perfect ones, and every bough on it will be like old-fashioned fans wide open. . . .

There will be a lot of aunts in the house. . . . Aunts of every complexion and cut. Christmas is the one time that even the most dubious of aunts takes on value. One of them can make up wreaths, another can make rock candy that puts a tremble on the heart, and still another can steer your twelve-seater bobsled—and turn it over, bottom up, with you all in just the right place for a fine spill.

There will be uncles, too, to hold one end of the molasses taffy you will pull sooner or later, yanking it out till it flashes and turns into cornsilk that almost floats in the air, tossing your end of it back and probably lassoing your uncle around his neck as you do it, and pulling out a new rope of solid honey. . . .

There will be cousins by the cart load. He-ones and she-ones. The size you can sit on, and the size that can sit on you. Enough for two armies, on Little Round Top and on Big, up in the haymow. You will play Gettysburg there till your heads are full of hay chaff that will keep six aunts busy

Photograph © Brad Simmons/Beateworks/Corbis

cleaning it out. And then you will come into the house and down a whole crock of molasses cookies—the kind that go up in peaks in the middle—which somebody was foolish enough to leave the cover off. . . .

The whole nation of you in the house will go from one thing to another. The secret of the best Christmases is everybody doing the same things all at the same time. You will all fall to and string cranberries and popcorn for the tree, and the bright lines each of you has a hold on will radiate from the tree like ribbons on a maypole. Everybody will have needles and thread in the mouth, you will all get in each other's way, but that is the art of doing Christmas right. . . .

But the pith of the party is not reached until the whole nation of you sits down in rocking chairs or lies down on their bellies in front of the six-foot gulf of fireplace. The presents are all stowed, heaped and tucked away, stuck fast with cornballs. The last lamps are out. The firelight dances on the ceiling. . . .

Then you had best find a fair substitute for my father. Give him the best chair in the house—and the way to find that is to push the cat out of it. . . . The firelight will get into your father's eyes and on his hair. . . . And you will hug your knees and hear the wind outside going its rounds among the snowy pines, and you will listen on till the story you are hearing becomes a part of the old winds of the world and the motion of the bright stars. And probably it will take two uncles at least to carry you to bed.

Home for Christmas

Garnett Ann Schultz

There's a friendly sort of feeling
With the ground so fresh and white,
Wreaths of holly in the windows,
And the tree all shining bright;
Turkey roasting in the oven,
And a welcome on the door—
All is well, you're home for Christmas
With the folks that you adore.

How you love the little children
As they hurry here and there,
With their little eyes just beaming
As they do their precious share.
Could they be such perfect angels
(Never seemed so good before)?
They are pleased you're home
    for Christmas,
And they meet you at the door.

Home for Christmas, nothing like it,
Just the greatest time of all,
With a million dreams to treasure
And a memory to recall.
All the family there about you,
Each one in the same old place;
You are home, and it is Christmas;
Smiles of gladness light each face.

Being Dad on Christmas Eve

Edgar A. Guest

They've hung their stockings up with care,
And I am in my old armchair,
And Mother's busy dragging out
The parcels hidden all about.
Within a corner, gaunt to see,
There stands a barren Christmas tree,
But soon upon its branches green
A burst of splendor will be seen.
And when the busy tongues grow still
That now are wagging with a will
Above me as I sit and rest,
I shall be at my happiest.
The greatest joy man can receive
Is being Dad on Christmas Eve.

Soon I shall toil with tinsel bright,
Place here and there a colored light;
And wheresoe'er my fingers lie,
Tomorrow shall a youngster spy
Some wonder gift or magic toy
To fill his little soul with joy.
The stockings on the mantelpiece
I'll bulge with sweets till every crease
That marks them now is stretched away.
There will be horns and drums to play
And dolls to love. For it's my task
To get for them the joys they ask.
What greater charm can fortune weave
Than being Dad on Christmas Eve?

With all their pomp, great monarchs miss
The happiness of scenes like this.
Rich halls tonight are still and sad
Because no little girl or lad
Shall wake upon the morn to find
The joys that love has left behind.
Oh, I have had my share of woe—
Known what it is to bear a blow—
Shed sorrow's tears, and stood to care
When life seemed desolate and bare;
Yet here tonight I smile and say
Worthwhile was all that came my way.
For this one joy, all else I'd leave:
To be their Dad on Christmas Eve.

Moving Christmas

Pamela Kennedy

I have a new respect for the Magi. You know, those guys who packed up their camels and headed out without any form of GPS more sophisticated than "following yonder star." I read somewhere that their trip took over a year. Imagine deciding what to take! Smart of them to pack gifts that didn't require much space—gold, frankincense, and myrrh. But how many changes of cloaks did they bring? What about turbans or accessories? It had to be wrenching to leave their books and astrological accoutrements behind. No room for those on a camel!

My fresh admiration for these ancient Middle Eastern travelers stems from my own recent activities. The children are grown and gone, setting up their own nests in far-flung cities. The family pet has passed on to her eternal reward. The career is coming to a close, and it's time to downsize as we move from our house into a condo. Don't get me wrong. I like the sound of the word. It makes me feel contemporary, frugal, and slender all at the same time. "Yes, we're downsizing!" I say, as if we're on a happy campaign. But the reality of downsizing is that to become what it sounds like, you actually have to make some serious decisions about getting rid of things and basically say "goodbye" to parts of your past.

Some decisions are easy. I never really liked that old, overstuffed chair or the framed print of the four-masted schooner. But other choices are more difficult. How many of Grandma's painted plates should we keep? And what about the hundreds of photos of us on vacation?

Then I come to the Christmas decor. I count out a dozen handmade gingham stars trimmed with tiny rickrack. They are a bit crooked, and the stitches aren't even. My mother sewed them as she sat outside the hospital delivery suite while I labored giving birth to our son. Mother is gone now, and our son is thirty-four. There's an angel made of macaroni that our eldest created in kindergarten and a reindeer crafted from a clothespin by our daughter in first grade. The hand-painted globe my father gave us on our first anniversary nestles in a box beside a delicate porcelain angel my husband brought from overseas. One by one, I remove treasured memories from the plastic storage boxes labeled "Christmas." By the time my husband returns, I am sitting on the floor surrounded by ornaments, needlepoint wall hangings, embroidered stockings, candles, a variety of Nativity characters, and a felt tree skirt embellished with crystal beads and sequins. Next to me, sitting empty, are two large bags labeled "toss" and "give away." After hours, I have found nothing in either category.

"Hey," he asks cheerfully, "how's the down-sizing going?"

I look at him, and tears fill my eyes. I can't speak past the lump in my throat, so I offer him what I have in my hand—a small stuffed angel with blue button eyes and tousled blonde hair. It reminds me of our daughter.

He takes the angel and looks at the mess on the floor. Then he begins to methodically repack everything into the large plastic cartons. He is quick and efficient, and before long everything is back in its place.

"What are you doing?" I finally ask as he stacks the cartons one upon the other. "What about downsizing?"

He helps me to my feet, brushes some glitter from my hair, and smiles. "Don't worry about it baby; this year we're moving Christmas."

Trim Your Tree

Ward Lamphere

Choose the finest tree of all—
Beautiful and straight and tall,
Sturdy trunk and shape so fine,
Fluffy branches, scent of pine.

String the lights and make them glow,
And hang the ornaments just so.
Recall the Babe born away so far,
And place upon the tree your star.

Trim your tree with joy this year.
Sing your song of Christmas cheer.
Raise your voice with all your might.
Hope the world will see the light.

Trim your tree with hope this year
That Christmas wishes will appear.

The star atop the tree so bright
Shows that love will make things right.

Trim your tree with peace this year.
May nations near and far from here
See the star above tonight
And finally, truly, end their fight.

Trim your tree with love this year.
Spread it thick to friends so dear,
And family who are out of sight,
Plus those we see each blessed night.

May joy and hope stream from above
And fill our hearts with peace and love.
Much better all our lives will be
If you trim your world just like your tree.

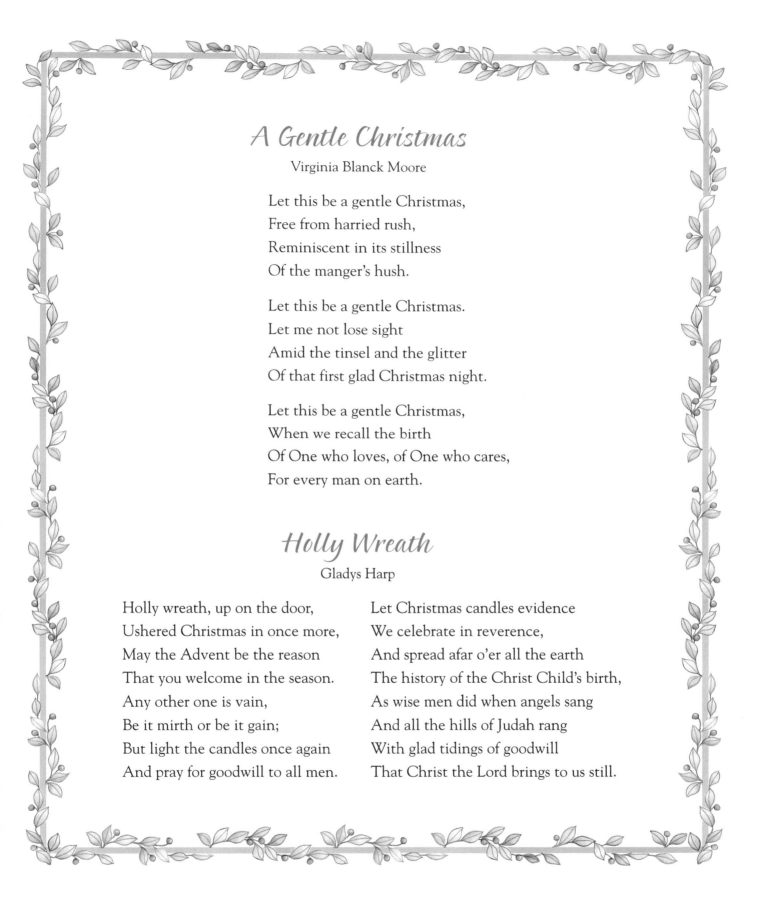

A Gentle Christmas

Virginia Blanck Moore

Let this be a gentle Christmas,
Free from harried rush,
Reminiscent in its stillness
Of the manger's hush.

Let this be a gentle Christmas.
Let me not lose sight
Amid the tinsel and the glitter
Of that first glad Christmas night.

Let this be a gentle Christmas,
When we recall the birth
Of One who loves, of One who cares,
For every man on earth.

Holly Wreath

Gladys Harp

Holly wreath, up on the door,
Ushered Christmas in once more,
May the Advent be the reason
That you welcome in the season.
Any other one is vain,
Be it mirth or be it gain;
But light the candles once again
And pray for goodwill to all men.

Let Christmas candles evidence
We celebrate in reverence,
And spread afar o'er all the earth
The history of the Christ Child's birth,
As wise men did when angels sang
And all the hills of Judah rang
With glad tidings of goodwill
That Christ the Lord brings to us still.

Unusual Christmas Gifts

Georgia B. Adams

I'm wrapping up some different gifts
At Christmastime this year;
Besides the gifts most usual
I'm tying up some cheer.

I'm taking it to one shut in,
In wrappings bright and gay,
I'm wrapping up some happiness
To brighten someone's day.

I'll take a heaping measure
Of warm faith and bits of joy
For family and friends of mine,
For smallest girl and boy.

I'll take some stardust and a dream
For that loved one of mine;
I'll even wrap a kiss or two
Along with love divine.

And then I'll wrap up months of hope,
Twelve months, in fact, 'twill be
(To last till Christmas comes again),
And give the gift from me!

A Joyful Noise

Faith Andrews Bedford

Every year, just before Christmas, I travel to New England to visit my aunt and nourish my Yankee roots with a bit of snow.

Aunt Nancy lives in a little village that is still mostly farms and orchards. Her house, built in 1776, is a warren of tiny rooms. Sheep graze in her meadows. Last night the sound of their bells lulled me to sleep.

When I came down for breakfast this morning, a cheery fire was crackling in the kitchen hearth, and the sound of music filled the house. More than fifty years ago her grandfather gave Aunt Nancy a piano when she graduated from college. She has given lessons ever since.

This morning the first student was playing ragtime. As I sipped my tea, my toe tapped time on the wide pine floorboards of the kitchen. Now, after a day of work and meetings in Boston, I've retreated with a good book to a cozy corner of Aunt Nancy's parlor. The December twilight gathers outside the windows, and a heavy snow has begun to fall. From the music room comes Aunt Nancy's voice counting time to a piece of music.

Suddenly the front door opens; a little girl enters amidst a swirl of snowflakes. Hanging up her jacket, she is soon sprawled on the braided rug in front of the fire, doing a puzzle. The music in the next room stops and Aunt Nancy bids farewell to a young man, then beckons to the little girl. I wonder what carol I will hear next. Thus far, I've listened to a very rapid "Good King Wenceslas," a halting "Deck the Halls," and an excellent "Silent Night."

At breakfast, Aunt Nancy told me that next Sunday will be her annual Christmas party. It is a time of music and singing for the children only. Parents are not invited. Aunt Nancy has been baking all week laying in a supply of Christmas goodies. Colorful cookie tins are piled high on the sideboard. The party is not a recital, she asserts, it's her Christmas gift to her students, a way of thanking them for their hard work.

"Years ago they used to bring me little presents," she said. "But I told them that I really only wanted one thing."

"And what is that?" I asked.

"One piece of music, perfectly played," she replied.

I look up from my book as the front door opens and a young woman comes in brushing snow from her hair. She nods a quiet greeting and picks up a book of poetry from the coffee table.

Presently, the last strains of "We Three Kings" fade away and the door to the studio opens. The little girl runs to her mother.

"Hi," Aunt Nancy says giving the young woman an affectionate hug and turns to me. "Dawn was one of my first students," she says, introducing us. "Now her daughters are following in her footsteps; I'm teaching all three." She pats the little girl's shoulder. "This is Anna. Molly and Ella come tomorrow."

While I help Aunt Nancy prepare supper, she speaks with pride of her past students and how some have gone on to careers in music. As she bastes the chicken, I reflect on how closely her life has been woven into the fabric of this tiny community and how far its thread reaches beyond the old stone walls that form its tidy borders.

In the summers, she and a group of friends bring homeless people out from Boston, sharing with them the peace of the country. Her house has always been the neighborhood repository for old clothes destined for homeless shelters and overseas missions. On Sunday evenings, she visits the local jail and plays with the prisoners' children so that they may have a bit of quiet time with their wives. To her, no one in this town is a stranger.

I see her touch everywhere in the village. The wonderful new school is a result of Aunt Nancy's many years on the School Board. She was a Girl Scout leader for more than thirty years, long after her daughters left home. And, as if six children of her own were not enough, she also hosted foreign students.

She will never retire. When someone broaches the subject, she looks stricken and says, "But who would teach the children?" Her energy is an inspiration.

During supper the phone rings. I hear Aunt Nancy speaking of wise men and shepherds. Returning to the table, she tells me that her church's Christmas pageant is only two weeks away.

After we do the dishes, we walk up to the village common, shuffling through the drifts. Sparkling snowflakes make haloes around the streetlamps.

"There's the village tree," Aunt Nancy says, pointing to a tall spruce set up on the village green. "When Dawn was studying with me, she played for the pageant," she recalls with pride. "This year her daughter Ella will play."

Photograph © Yu Lan/Shutterstock Images

Last year my visit coincided with the festivities. Although each church has its own pageant, they all finished at the same time. Church doors opened wide, flooding the snow with golden light from their sanctuaries. Families poured down the steps pulling on mittens. Excited children raced toward the tree. Here and there a dog scampered through the crowd. As the common began to fill, people joined hands around the tree. Suddenly its lights blazed on; a small brass band struck up the first carol. The singing began, hesitant at first, then stronger. A joyful noise filled the air as every voice was lifted in song.

This year, as in decades past, Aunt Nancy will look around the circle and see many of her students, past and present, young and old. There will undoubtedly be some former Girl Scouts; perhaps a prisoner's family will come to seek a bit of cheer on this festive night. The thread of her caring and her music binds them together. The common will be filled by those whose lives have been touched by half a century of her giving. But Aunt Nancy would say that it is she who has received the gifts.

Christmas Melodies

Linda C. Grazulis

Hallelujah! Christmas has arrived
As the joyous laughter rings,
From the snowy ice-capped mountains
To the cozy homes where boisterous
        children sing.
Hear the cheery sounds of sleigh bells
As horses trot knees deep in snow—
Listen to family, friends, and neighbors,
Chitchatting with happy hearts aglow.
Oh, hear the bongs of silver bells ringing
On a steeple tower high,
While holy hymns are flowing like a river
As spirits take to wing and fly!
For there's nothing quite like Christmas
With tenors, a cappella, bass,
And the bellow of a baritone
Singing of God's love and grace.

*The Christmas tree in Rockefeller Center, New York City,
New York. Photograph © Robert Harding Picture
Library/SuperStock*

This Is the Night

Author Unknown

This is the night
When all our finest art
Pales before the beauty
Of a single shining star.

This is the night
When all of our profoundest symphonies
Fade beneath the swelling
Of a simple angel song.

This is the night
When all the badges of office
Are smothered in the folds
Of a rough-woven tunic
And the scepters of power give way
To a humble shepherd's staff.

This is the night
When man's swiftest wheels and wings
Prove far inadequate;
And he treads, instead, the path
Of a camel caravan.

This is the night
When the unkind act is frozen still
And is buried in the desert sand—
When the first sharp word falls soundlessly
And is swallowed by the desert air.

This is the night
When princes and kings and presidents
Make one obeisance;
When diplomats forsake finesse
And ministers, their chambers;
When a worried world abandons argument
And breathes its plea for peace
In the quiet of a stable.

Photograph © John Dorado/Shutterstock Images

Christmas List

Lucile Davis

Tomorrow will be Christmas Day.
I'll just recheck my list,
Go over every item
So that nothing will be missed.

The tree is trimmed, the stockings hung,
The presents wrapped with care.
Aunt Emma's gift is in the mail
With lots of time to spare.

The kitchen boasts of its bounty;
We've hung the mistletoe.
The holly wreath is on the door,
Complete with festive bow.

Why do I have the feeling
That my list is not complete?
Then I recall that holy night
And kneel at Jesus' feet.

The family gathers round to hear
The story of His birth,
Of how God loved the world so much,
He sent His Son to earth.

We join the shepherds in the field;
We hear the angels sing.
The baby born in Bethlehem
Is Jesus Christ, our King.

We kneel down with the wise men
To worship and adore.
The manger holds the hope of
Humankind forevermore.

With joyful thanks we rise to savor
Every Christmas treat.
His spirit fills our hearts with love;
My list is now complete.

A Nativity Song

Frances Chesterton

How far is it to Bethlehem?
Not very far.
Shall we find the stable room
Lit by a star?

Can we see the little Child,
Is He within?
If we lift the wooden latch,
May we go in?

May we stroke the
    creatures there—
Ox, ass, or sheep?
May we peep like them
And see Jesus asleep?

If we touch His tiny hand,
Will He awake?

Will He know we've come so far
Just for His sake?

Great kings have precious gifts,
And we have naught.
Little smiles and little tears
Are all we brought.

For all weary children,
Mary must weep;
Here, on His bed of straw,
Sleep, children, sleep.

God in His mother's arms,
Babes in the byre,
Sleep, as they sleep who find
Their heart's desire.

Christmas in the Country

Ralph W. Seager

Everywhere, everywhere, Christmas tonight," yet nowhere is it more beautifully simple than in the country. To the everlasting glory of innkeepers everywhere, the one in Luke saw to it that Mary knew her time in the midst of things of home—country things. He was the fourth wise man and the wisest of all.

Surely the clean straw, the warmth of cattle, and the soft bleating of the sheep had the best to offer to this night. Where else could shepherd boys have knelt with kings? Where else could doves and donkeys have been so well at home? Where else a better place for the good Shepherd than among the lambs? Small wonder, when a young, fleecy head came under her hand, that

Mary looked to her own child and murmured, "Lamb."

There were crickets at her feet and the velvet cheek of the ox at her shoulder, watching over her. The bull and the ox take the privilege of custody upon themselves when it comes to babes and children. Farmers have told me that their infant child is the safest member of the family around the bull. It may be that some strange, yet holy heritage has come down to them from the Christmas stable.

I witnessed this strange heritage once, at the State Fair. There stood the vast and arrogant bull, shackles on his feet, his nose ringed and chained. Bovine and behemoth, he towered in majesty above all of his kindred kine. Pitchfork guardians,

alert to his great strength, were with him constantly. Evidently there was basis for apprehension on their part.

Now comes the miracle I have since come to accept. A small boy, a toddler, walked along between the iron stanchions and then stopped by this bull. The boy patted his hand against the heavy rods, while from his child's throat came diminutive sounds in his own private language. I was tempted to draw him away, but something held my hand back; anyway, the pen separated them safely.

The child thrust his hand between the bars trying to touch that massive beast, but he could not reach so high. Then the enormous head lowered, and the bull came down on his knees, pressing his face to the barricade. The child cooed with glee as he fondled that monstrous, yet noble head. I watched enthralled; it was a lovely scene.

At the risk of skepticism, I must go on to say that I saw a glistening, a moistness, come into the glance of this creature. Whatever else it could have been, something much like weeping filled his plum eyes. Of course, an arm-jerking mother came along and dragged the child away on the backs of his heels.

I turned to the pitchforkers and asked whether the child was familiar to the bull. "No," they answered. "He's never seen him before."

From barn to meadow, valley to mountain, the countryside is the Creator's best witness of His goodwill to His children. Here is man's first and ultimate home, where he knows compassion in the shelter of great oaks and in the touch of beasts.

Barn in LaSalle County, Illinois. Photograph © Mary Liz Austin/Donnelly-Austin Photography

What Does Joe Do?

Louisa Godissart McQuillen

The day was cold and snowy, and it was also my daughter Erin's birthday. To celebrate, her husband, Tim, was taking her to the Penn State evening football game. They left me, "Nanny," in charge of my three-year-old grandson. I bundled J.P. into his warm jacket, and we went "Christmas-looking."

Soon, we were standing in front of Philipsburg's True Value hardware store, gazing at an almost life-size Nativity display through the showcase windows. Mary, Joseph, and the Christ Child looked real enough to speak as we solemnly observed them from the opposite side of the huge glass. They seemed to overwhelm J.P., who had seen only miniature versions of the familiar Christmas scene. He stared at the Babe for a moment, and then started firing questions at me.

"Who's that, Nanny?"

I leaned down to his level and looked him in the eye.

"Why, that's Baby Jesus," I said. "Don't you remember?"

He looked at the young woman kneeling before the manger.

"Who's that one?" he wanted to know. Now I was a bit amused.

"That's Mary, Jesus' mommy."

J.P. looked higher. His eyes paused on the bearded face of the father figure. Then he slowly looked down, down, down—past the man's walking staff, past his long brown robe—clear down to his sandaled feet. J.P. stood quietly, his little mittened hands hanging limply at his sides.

Hmm, I thought, he might need some help here. "And that's Joseph, Jesus' daddy!" I said firmly, knowing that I had mentioned the entire family now, so that should take care of any curiosity this child had left!

J.P. seemed to be thoughtful as he stared up at the tall figure standing protectively over his family. Suddenly he looked up at me, and in a soft voice he asked, "What does Joe do?"

"What?" I asked, startled by his informal naming of Mary's husband. I wasn't sure I had heard him right.

"What does Joe do, Nanny?"

I laughed, but J.P. was serious. Perhaps he was comparing Jesus' earthly father with his own. J.P.'s daddy wears a gun and holster, however, not a walking staff. Tim is a state policeman, and his gray uniform and tall black boots must have seemed far removed from Joseph's flowing robes and sandaled feet!

I thought about the words that sprang from the insquisitive three-year-old's heart: "What does Joe do, Nanny?"

I knew God chose Joseph to be His Son Jesus' stepfather. Yet I wondered if this biblical explanation might be difficult for a small child to grasp. So standing in front of the store's showcase window that cold night, I told JP in simple terms how "Joe" fit into the Christmas story.

His question was as old as Mary and Joseph themselves and perhaps as confusing to them back then as it was to JP this snowy winter night. Besides the fact that family lineage gave him proper credentials, just what did Joe do?

Could it simply be spiritual obedience that made him stand head and shoulders above other men in God's sight? God knew Joseph's heart. The carpenter was an honest, gentle, and mature man who would love and care for Mary and the child. He was trustworthy and faithful. Above all, he deeply loved God.

Joseph could have ignored the voice urging him to marry the young girl. He could also have talked himself out of the marriage, since his friends and neighbors all knew Mary's condition and no doubt questioned his intent to marry her.

What would we have said if Joseph was our friend and told us

Photograph © Alexander Hoffmann/Shutterstock Images

his intended wife carried another's child? Perhaps they said it too: "Surely you jest, Joe! Wake up and smell the coffee, man!"

Joseph must have been confused. Surely he asked himself many questions. Regardless, he obeyed when the angel directed him to marry her.

Mary's beloved was visited in a dream by an angel of God and heeded the dream's warning: He rushed his little family into Egypt, where they lived until it was safe to return home.

Time after time Joseph followed God's lead-

ing, straight and true, like an arrow follows an unseen path from the bow that releases it. In fact, that's how I answered J.P.'s question:

"What does Joe do, J.P.? He obeys God. Joe's like a straight arrow, and we should all try to be more like him!"

My answer must have satisfied the little guy. He stuffed one hand deep into his jacket pocket. With the other, he led me, grinning, into the warmth of the store to look at toys.

Featured Poet

Imagine the Stable

Eileen Spinelli

Imagine how it was—
stable luminous in starry light,
shepherds steeped in a night
all dizzy with grace.

Imagine the warm,
sweet-grass place
where the baby lay asleep—
the singing of angels
and rapturous birds,
their glad words
stirring even
the sheep.

Imagine the footfalls
of camels,
the heartbeat
of kings
stumbling east
toward a miracle.

Imagine how it was—
breeze wafting wonder
and peace
and gladness
across valley and hill.

Imagine
how it could be . . .
could be
still.

The Landlord Speaks

Amos Russell Wells

What could be done? The inn was full of folks!
His honor, Marcus Lucius, and his scribes
Who made the census: honorable men
From farthest Galilee, come hitherward
To be enrolled; high ladies and their lords;
The rich, the rabbis, such a noble throng
As Bethlehem had never seen before
And may not see again. And there they were,
Close-herded with their servants, till the inn
Was like a hive at swarming-time, and I
Was fairly crazed among them.

    Could I know
That they were so important? Just the two,
No servants, just a workman sort of man,
Leading a donkey, and his wife theron
Drooping and pale . . . I saw them not myself,
My servants must have driven them away;
But had I seen them, how was I to know?
Were inns to welcome stragglers, up and down
In all our towns from Beersheba to Dan,
Till He should come? And how were men to know?

There was a sign, they say, a heavenly light
Resplendent: but I had no time for stars,
And there were songs of angels in the air
Out on the hills; but how was I to hear
Amid the thousand clamors of an inn?
Of course, if I had known them, who they were,
And who was He that should be born that night,
For now I learn that they will make him King,
A second David, who will ransom us
From these Philistine Romans . . . who but He
That feeds an army with a loaf of bread,

And if a soldier falls, He touches him
And up he leaps, uninjured? Had I known
I would have turned the whole inn upside down,
His honor, Marcus Lucius, and the rest,
And sent them all to the stables, had I known.

So you have seen Him, stranger, and perhaps
Again may see Him? Prithee say for me,
I did not know; and if He comes again
As He will surely come, with retinue,
And banners, and an army, tell my Lord
That all my inn is His to make amends.

Alas! Alas! to miss a chance like that!
This inn that might be chief among them all,
The birthplace of Messiah . . .
    had I known!

Joseph's Dream
Matthew 1:18–25

Now the birth of Jesus Christ was on this wise: When as his mother Mary was espoused to Joseph, before they came together, she was found with child of the Holy Ghost.

Then Joseph her husband, being a just man, and not willing to make her a public example, was minded to put her away privily.

But while he thought on these things, behold, the angel of the Lord appeared unto him in a dream, saying, Joseph, thou son of David, fear not to take unto thee Mary thy wife: for that which is conceived in her is of the Holy Ghost.

And she shall bring forth a son, and thou shalt call his name Jesus: for he shall save his people from their sins.

Now all this was done, that it might be fulfilled which was spoken of the Lord by the prophet, saying, Behold, a virgin shall be with child, and shall bring forth a son, and they shall call his name Emmanuel, which being interpreted is, God with us.

Then Joseph being raised from sleep did as the angel of the Lord had bidden him, and took unto him his wife: And knew her not till she had brought forth her firstborn son: and he called his name Jesus.

The Birth and Presentation at the Temple
Luke 2:4–7, 22, 25–35

And Joseph also went up from Galilee, out of the city of Nazareth, into Judaea, unto the city of David, which is called Bethlehem; (because he was of the house and lineage of David:) To be taxed with Mary his espoused wife, being great with child.

And so it was, that, while they were there, the days were accomplished that she should be delivered. And she brought forth her firstborn son, and wrapped him in swaddling clothes, and laid him in a manger; because there was no room for them in the inn. . . .

And when the days of her purification according to the law of Moses were accomplished, they brought him to Jerusalem, to present him to the Lord. . . .

And, behold, there was a man in Jerusalem, whose name was Simeon; and the same man was just and devout, waiting for the consolation of Israel: and the Holy Ghost was upon him. And it was revealed unto him by the Holy Ghost, that he should not see death, before he had seen the Lord's Christ.

And he came by the Spirit into the temple: and when the parents brought in the child Jesus, to do for him after the custom of the law, Then took he him up in his arms, and blessed God, and said, Lord, now lettest thou thy servant depart in peace, according to thy word:

For mine eyes have seen thy salvation, Which thou hast prepared before the face of all people; A light to lighten the Gentiles, and the glory of thy people Israel.

And Joseph and his mother marvelled at those things which were spoken of him.

And Simeon blessed them, and said unto Mary his mother, Behold, this child is set for the fall and rising again of many in Israel; and for a sign which shall be spoken against; (Yea, a sword shall pierce through thy own soul also,) that the thoughts of many hearts may be revealed.

Herod and the Flight to Egypt

Matthew 2:1–15

Now when Jesus was born in Bethlehem of Judaea in the days of Herod the king, behold, there came wise men from the east to Jerusalem, Saying, Where is he that is born King of the Jews? for we have seen his star in the east, and are come to worship him.

When Herod the king had heard these things, he was troubled, and all Jerusalem with him. And when he had gathered all the chief priests and scribes of the people together, he demanded of them where Christ should be born.

And they said unto him, In Bethlehem of Judaea: for thus it is written by the prophet, And thou Bethlehem, in the land of Juda, art not the least among the princes of Juda: for out of thee shall come a Governor, that shall rule my people Israel.

Then Herod, when he had privily called the wise men, enquired of them diligently what time the star appeared. And he sent them to Bethlehem, and said, Go and search diligently for the young child; and when ye have found him, bring me word again, that I may come and worship him also.

When they had heard the king, they departed; and, lo, the star, which they saw in the east, went before them, till it came and stood over where the young child was. When they saw the star, they rejoiced with exceeding great joy.

And when they were come into the house, they saw the young child with Mary his mother, and fell down, and worshipped him: and when they had opened their treasures, they presented unto him gifts; gold, and frankincense and myrrh.

And being warned of God in a dream that they should not return to Herod, they departed into their own country another way.

And when they were departed, behold, the angel of the Lord appeareth to Joseph in a dream, saying, Arise, and take the young child and his mother, and flee into Egypt, and be thou there until I bring thee word: for Herod will seek the young child to destroy him.

When he arose, he took the young child and his mother by night, and departed into Egypt:

And was there until the death of Herod: that it might be fulfilled which was spoken of the Lord by the prophet, saying, Out of Egypt have I called my son.

The Message of the Stars

Edith S. Butler

*E*ver since the creation of the human race, the stars have held a mystery and a challenge for the mind of man; and his eyes have been lifted upward from his earth to their beauty until they became a symbol of faith and hope in the darkness.

For it is written that in the beginning God made the stars and set them in the firmament of heaven to give light upon the earth.

And again it is written that the Lord spoke to Job out of the whirlwind, saying, "Where wast thou when I laid the foundations of the earth? declare, if thou hast understanding. . . . when the morning stars sang together, and all the sons of God shouted for joy?" (Job 38:4, 7)

The psalmist sang, "The heavens declare the glory of God; and the firmament sheweth his handywork" (Psalm 19:1). There is great beauty and majesty in these timeless words.

Through the ages many others have written regarding these celestial bodies. Ralph Waldo Emerson said, "If stars should appear one night in a thousand years, how would men believe and adore; and preserve for many generations the remembrance of the city of God which had been shown! But every night come out these envoys of beauty, and light the universe with their admonishing smile."

In these words, John Milton expressed his thoughts: "The stars that nature hung in heaven and filled their lamps with everlasting oil, give due light to the misled and lonely traveler." . . .

At Christmastime, more than any other season, perhaps, we look to the heavens and we think of the great Star of the East which led the wise men to the Babe of Bethlehem. "When they saw the star, they rejoiced with exceeding great joy" (Matthew 2:10).

From the first chapter of Genesis to the final chapter of Revelation, the stars are mentioned time and time again, and it is written in almost the last words of this greatest of all books that Jesus said, "I am the root and the offspring of David, and the bright and morning star" (Revelation 22:16).

Northern lights over outdoor Nativity set in Alberta, Canada.
Photograph © age fotostock/SuperStock

Softly the Night Is Sleeping

Author Unknown

Softly the night is sleeping on Bethlehem's peaceful hill,
Silent the shepherds watching their gentle flocks are still.
But hark the wondrous music falls from the opening sky,
Valley and cliff re-echo glory to God on high.
Glory to God it rings again,
Peace on earth, goodwill to men.

Come with the gladsome shepherds quick hastening from the fold,
Come with the wise men bringing incense and myrrh and gold,
Come to Him poor and lowly, all round the cradle throng,
Come with our hearts of sunshine and sing the angels' song.
Glory to God tell out again,
Peace on the earth, goodwill to men.

Wave ye the wreath unfading, the fir tree and the pine,
Green from the snows of winter to deck the holy shrine;
Bring ye the happy children for this is Christmas morn,
Jesus the sinless infant, Jesus the Lord is born.
Glory to God, to God again,
Peace on the earth, goodwill to men.

WE ASK FOR GENTLENESS,
Dear God, this Christmas,
For kindliness and sympathy and mirth;
For courage to walk proudly to high music
That sings again above the dreaming earth.
Oh, may we have that faith deep-planted in us
That life is good if we keep tryst with Thee . . .
God, give us songs of peace, of hope and courage,
To sing this year around the Christmas tree!

—HELEN WELSHIMER

The Story of a Song

Epiphany Gift

Pamela Kennedy

While most of us exchange Christmas gifts on December 24 or 25, there are those who choose to wait until Epiphany on January 6, a date traditionally celebrated as the time when the Magi presented gifts to the young Jesus.

It was out of this tradition that the carol "We Three Kings of Orient Are" was written by American author and composer John Henry Hopkins Jr. Born in Pittsburgh, Pennsylvania, in 1820, John was both bright and hardworking. By the age of thirty he had graduated from New York's General Theology Seminary and established himself as a professional writer, founding *The Church Journal* and later publishing a book titled *Carols, Hymns, and Songs.*

The composition of this beloved Christmas carol was, however, more of a personal endeavor. Although single, John Hopkins loved spending holidays with his nephews and nieces. In the Episcopal tradition, they exchanged gifts on January 6 in celebration of Epiphany. In 1857, while reading the second chapter of Matthew's gospel, Hopkins meditated upon the account of the Magi coming to visit the young Jesus. Using his knowledge of biblical history and secular literature, as well as his love of music, he decided to create a new hymn for the children based upon the journey of these ancient travelers from the East.

In his brilliant retelling he uses evocative language to describe their trek over "field and fountain, moor and mountain, following yonder star," then weds his words to a melody that mimics the rhythmic gait of a camel caravan. Always the teacher, he also weaves threads of Christian doctrine into the second through fifth verses connecting each gift to an aspect of Christ's ministry. The gold is a gift fit for a king, recalling the scriptural prophecy that the Messiah would be from David's kingly line. The gift of frankincense, an aromatic resin used as incense, is a symbol of prayer and Christ's deity as the Son of God. The third gift, myrrh, commonly used in embalming, speaks of the Savior's sacrificial death for mankind. In the final verse, Hopkins changes the somber tone of the poem to one of victory as heaven and earth sing "Alleluia" to the risen Savior who is king, God, and sacrifice.

Intended as a gift for his young nieces and nephews, Hopkins, in fact, created a gift for millions who would follow after them. Sung around the world each year at both Christmas and Epiphany, this hymn reaffirms the journey of all those who still seek, and find, in Christ, "God's perfect light."

We Three Kings of Orient Are

Lyrics and Music by John Henry Hopkins Jr.

Christmas Dawning
Carol Bessent Hayman

Another Christmas dawning,
Shepherds on hillsides far
Marveled at angels singing
And one bright shining star.

Now on this Christmas morning,
Savior, my heart I bring.
Lo, how the star is shining!
Hear how the angels sing.

Take Time
This Christmas Day
James Dillet Freeman

Take time this Christmas Day to go
A little way apart
And with the hands of prayer prepare
The house that is your heart.

Brush out the dusty fears, brush out
The cobwebs of your care,
Till in the house that is your heart
It's Christmas everywhere.

Light every window up with love,
And let your love shine through,
That they who walk outside may share
The blessed light with you.

Then will the rooms with joy be bright,
With peace the hearth be blessed,
And Christ Himself will enter in
To be your Christmas Guest.

Peaceful, Peaceful Christmas Day

Keith H. Graham

Tiny snowflakes swirl softly down,
dressing pine trees in diamond gowns.
Gathering in silence in glistening mounds,
they ignite rare beauty across barren ground.

So, wander much, daydream, and play!
It's peaceful, peaceful Christmas Day!

Young children romp here and there,
sporting red cheeks and snow-speckled hair.
Laughing, they sail without a care
upon sleek sleds to everywhere.

So, wander much, daydream, and play!
It's peaceful, peaceful Christmas Day!

Christmas Morning

Keith H. Graham

Quiet Christmas morning.
Silence whispers words
in fluffy flakes of snow
floating slowly downward
to the sleepy earth below.

Pretty Christmas morning.
Powdery snowdrifts sparkle
in a picture-perfect scene;
red and green lights twinkle
on a snowy evergreen.

Merry Christmas morning.
People sing as laughter rings
from little girls and boys

unwrapping ribboned gifts,
discovering wished-for toys.

Wondrous Christmas morning.
Wonders untold unfold
at God's steady command
painting hope-framed pictures
in a sometimes
        hope-starved land.

God's Christmas morning.
He creates the miracles in many
sparkles and hues,
and by baby Jesus says,
"Rejoice! I love you!"

Christmastide

Ella Weber Walker

As life goes on, through smiles and tears
Come happy thoughts of yesteryears;
Of family, home, and holidays
And Christmas with its merry ways;
Of lots of fun and lots of gifts,
And friends to share our happiness,
A holly wreath upon the door,
Plum pudding steamed the day before,
Red balls upon a Christmas tree
And tinsel decked so festively;
Of turkeys stuffed, and stockings hung;
Of dolls and sleigh and toy gun.
A wealth of memories . . . may these abide
With you at every Christmastide.

ISBN-13: 978-0-8249-1340-3

Published by Ideals Publications
A Guideposts Company
Nashville, Tennessee
www.idealsbooks.com

Publisher, Peggy Schaefer
Editor, Melinda L. R. Rumbaugh
Copy Editors, Debra Wright, Kaye Dacus
Designer, Marisa Jackson
Permissions Editor, Kristi West

Cover: Photograph © GAP Interiors/Dan Duchars
Inside front cover: *Christmas Eve* by Nicky Boehme. Image © Nicky Boehme/Art Licensing Int'l.
Inside back cover: *Cozy Christmas Cat* by Ruth Sanderson. Image © Ruth Sanderson
Art for "Bits & Pieces," "Family Recipes," back cover spot art, and spot art for pages 1, 58, and 64, by Dorian Lee Remine. "We Three Kings of Orient Are" sheet music by Dick Torrans, Melode, Inc.

Readers are invited to submit original poetry and prose for possible use in future publications. Please send no more than four typed submissions to: Magazine Submissions, Ideals Publications, 2630 Elm Hill Pike, Suite 100, Nashville, Tennessee 37214. Manuscripts will be returned if a self-addressed stamped envelope is included.

ACKNOWLEDGMENTS:

FREEMAN, JAMES DILLET. "Take Time This Christmas Day." Used with permission of Unity, www.unity.org. OUR THANKS to the following authors or their heirs: Faye Adams, Georgia B. Adams, Faith Andrews Bedford, Ruth M. Bryan, Edith S. Butler, Robert Tristram Coffin, Lucile Davis, Leslie-Leigh Ducros, Patricia Ann Emme, Loise Pinkerton Fritz, Keith H. Graham, Linda C. Grazulis, Edgar Guest, Nelle Hardgrove, Gladys Harp, Clay Harrison, Carol Bessent Hayman, Esther Hirst, Linda Ann Hughes, Pamela Kennedy, Ward Lamphere, Pamela Love, Alice Arlene MacCulloch, Louisa Godissart McQuillen, Isabel Miller, Claire Mitchell, Ruby Lee Mitchell, Patricia Mongeau, Virginia Blanck Moore, Garnett A. Schultz, Ralph W. Seager, Dorothy Cameron Smith, Eileen Spinelli, Ella Weber Walker, Helen Welshimer, and Horace Wilson.

Every effort has been made to establish ownership and use of each selection in this book. If contacted, the publisher will be pleased to rectify any inadvertent errors or omissions in subsequent printings.